CASCADE

Poetry from Foreshore

THE HAPPENING OF MAGIC

Phil M. Shirley was born in Stoke-on-Trent in 1965. He worked as a journalist and sportswriter and is the author of numerous books - biographies, essays and novels - including *The Rivers That Run Through Us* and *The Soul of Boxing*, longlisted for the William Hill Sports Book of the Year. He now lives in Kent.

ALSO BY PHIL M. SHIRLEY

The Rivers That Run Through Us
The Soul of Boxing
Blood & Thunder: The Unofficial Biography of Jonah Lomu
Deadly Obsessions: Life and Death in Formula One
Where is the Winning Post?: The biography of Mikie Heaton-Ellis
Hoddle: The Faith to Win
Miracles Can Happen
Gospel Behind Bars

PRAISE FOR PHIL M. SHIRLEY'S WRITING

The Rivers That Run Through Us

From Goodreads

'This novel hits your like a wave, a flood, a slap in the face: a dark dramatisation of violence that is as stark as it is poetic. I couldn't put it down. I wanted to, often, because many passages disturb the soul, upset the mind, but there is also the promise of redemption, hope - a light in the dark - and, surprisingly, moments that make you laugh. And then you want to take the book and throw it in the river, because the truth can be an awful weight and responsibility and this novel is both. The cast of characters will live with me a long time.' Lawrence Abrams.

'PHILLIP MICHAEL SHIRLEY has created a very good blend of literary fiction with stunning lyrical prose. I particularly love the character of Sunny - in my eyes the protagonist and the subject of the wonderful cover art. I was exhausted by the time the story climaxed and felt like crying, such was my emotional investment in the story. This is praise indeed for the author who knows how to write with impact, if not by the rules.' Julia Boyd.

'Phillip Michael Shirley writes from the heart with honesty and passion and courage: he pulls no punches with the dialogue. The prose is remarkable. The balance between reality and fantasy (or is it fantasy? Maybe not.) is amazingly well done. Reading this novel is like being having a deep dream and waking up and falling back into the dream, over and over again. Exhilarating.' Veronica Edward.

'A fantastic, impactful and powerful debut novel from an honest, journeyman writer who, I'm guessing, has lived a colourful life, such is the rich tapestry of characters and situations in this unique story. Highly recommended.' Rachel Coleman.

A beautifully written story. Very powerful, sometimes shocking and always page turning. The gritty reality and dream like surrealism work well together. It is incredibly well crafted and layered. I cried at the end. Can't remember when I last read a book that made me cry! The Rivers That Run Through Us is a rollercoaster of emotion. It touched me deeply. I doubt I will ever be able to forget this story. It could be classic.' Y F Chang.

'The presence of mythical creatures and the natural world intertwine with the human narratives, adding depth and a sense of the universal to the personal struggles. The story masterfully combines realism with myth and surrealism, offering a rich exploration of the complexities of human nature against the backdrop of an indifferent universe. This haunting tale leaves a lasting impression, challenging you to contemplate the possibility of redemption and the enduring power of the human spirit amidst the trials of life.' Gavin Johnson.

'Unforgettable characters, off-the-wall storytelling, and a refreshingly bad attitude to structure and violence. This novel manages to captivate, while offering a no-holds-barred exploration of human nature. The good, the bad and the ugly. The Rivers That Run Through Us is magic in the gutter of life. Love it and hate it. It's gutsy and utterly out-of-this-world.' Jerome Chen.

'The Rivers That Run Through Us is a compelling story centered on five brothers and their father, each from the same hellish upbringing and all thrust into the world virtually on their own. Each character embraces their new, dysfunctional freedom in different ways and shapes their lives with actions that intertwine, interfere, and overlap with each other. It's a revenge story, it's a survival story, and it's a grim yet engaging story about painful, tenuous, enduring family connections. I found the writing style to be brief, snappy, and evocative. Many of the descriptions and word choices were deeply profound and yet subtle enough to keep the pacing well balanced. The dialogue had a great deal of personality in it and each character shone through in their actions, word choices, and how they interacted with each other. It's a relatively short novel, but it never wastes a moment. There is a supernatural/metaphorical element to the story, represented by hares, foxes, and stags, some which talk and others which don't need words to convey the weight of their presence. There's suggestion of reincarnation and otherworldly will, and I enjoyed the subtle yet punchy presence of it. I enjoyed this novel and would recommend it to others who want an evocative, snappy, and mysterious story with great pacing, a wry sense of humor, and enough drama to keep you reading it well into the night.' Cheyenne DeBorde

'This is one of the best-written books I have read this year. There is something so special about the writing style, I can't really put it into words. I want to say masterpiece. I will say incredible.' Erik Larsen.

'The storyline is a masterclass in controlled madness. By that I mean it's chaos with a path to navigate. I even found the long sentences enjoyable and found myself reading some of them over and over again. I highly recommend this novel. It is, despite the unorthodox nature, fulfilling and unputdownable. A great experience.' Paul Cook.

PHILLIP M. SHIRLEY

The Happening of Magic

With an introduction by the author

FORESHORE PUBLISHING
LONDON

CASCADE
Foreshore Publishing
86-90 Paul Street London EC2A 4NE
www.foreshorepublishing.com

Cascade is an imprint of Foreshore Publishing Limited
Reg. No. 13358650

The Happening of Magic

Font ~ Minion
Typeset by Richard Powell
Printed and bound in Great Britain by 4Edge Ltd, Essex.

ISBN: 978-1-0686132-2-7

Contents

Introduction

This is the first collection of poetry I have had published, and possibly the last; a dramatic and arguably self-important statement from a lesser known writer and even lesser known poet, one whose work - of this discipline at least - is akin to a human giving birth to a monkey. What perversion has been done ? What madness unleashed on the world? What possessed one to experiment in such a way? Poetry... the Frankenstein of writing. A monstrous undertaking indeed. So why?

I wasn't inspired to start writing by any one incident or happening, at least I can't recall if this is true. I can remember, as a nine year-old at school, being compelled to write stories; the beginning of the passion, I guess. But, now, as this question focuses my mind on past experiences, as a traveller may squint at shapes down a fog shrouded road on a journey back home, I do recall a moment when I may have been inspired to become a writer, an author. The summer of 1976. I was ten years old. My English teacher recited parts of Jaws, the novel by American writer Peter Benchley, to an open-mouthed, wide-eyed class of children. We all wanted to look at the cover. I was impacted by the writing; the storytelling. I must also say that my mother used to read to me. Thomas Hardy and John Betjeman, the English poet. My late father was, I believe a frustrated author. Some years after he left, I discovered some of his writing; a short story about cows, if my memory serves me right. He became a salesman. It has been the experience of reading, with great appetite and desire, works of fiction by writers rather than life situations that has most influenced me. John Steinbeck, James Herbert, Cormac McCarthy, Arthur C. Clarke, H.P.Lovecraft, W.P. Kinsella, and the English poets Coleridge, Wordsworth, Byron, Shelley, Keats.

Shelley's sonnet Ozymandias made a huge impression on me as a young writer, as did the first poetry book I ever read - H'm by the Welsh writer and son of a sea captain R S Thomas; handed to me, along with a copy of Bruce Springsteen's Born to Run album, by the guy who ran the school youth club. One of those life changing happenings.

The cinema of rock 'n' roll. Soundtracks to life. The anger, darkness and pain of fractured lives, the beauty and the promise of escape. And the ethereal world. The hard balance. On one hand the mystic and the mystery and on the other the stark reality of humanity. Some of the themes in my work are based on my own life experiences. Semi-autobiographical elements. Writing fiction close to the truth of life is not only cathartic for the writer but, in my opinion, deeply resonating for the reader.

I have been very fortunate to have been able to work, for most of my life, as a writer - author, copywriter, journalist - among other things. I got a lucky break in my thirties when HarperCollins discovered my work and gave me a multi-book deal. But writing, as a discipline, does not come easy to me. The ideas never stop flowing. The writing process does, often. I think I'm lazy, easily distracted. I'm getting better, more disciplined, and learning how to get the words down quickly. I believe the enemy of the writer is perfectionism; the mother of all procrastination.

Poetry is a hard discipline to master. I shudder to think how many rules I may have broken in my clumsy attempt to create rhyme and reason and form. But, if there is beauty, humanity and nobility in standing in the wreckage of a screwed up life and telling true stories about how it all came to ruin, then there is some honour in having a go, as a writer, at poetry. The funniest thing I have ever seen is my ego and original belief system, born out of patterns and assumptions, dead beat, shocked and out for the count.

We are expendable. Our greatness is dust in the wind. But the really gratifying thing of being human is being able to boast of one's defeat, and laugh about it. Laugh at one's self, for being stupid to think we can engineer certainty. In the words of teacher, author, storyteller and spiritual activist Stephen Jenkinson "whatever is left standing - and there is always something left standing when you wrestle angels - is the thing that was true about you and your life all along, as faithful a companion as the Earth that will one day cradle you again.

Many of the poems in this collection were written between 2020 and 2023 when I lived by the River Thames in East London. Others came from different places and times.

Phil M. Shirley, April 2024.

for the kindness and softness
that comforts me
through the
madness.

i've been
sifting through the madness
for a good line.
last seen
soaked in alcohol
wasting time.
caught between
arcs and plots
out of my mind.
staring at the screen
waiting for worlds
to collide.

4AM

end of June
steel blue sky
pregnant with heat
prehistoric gulls
glide silent
in low haze
over faintly moving
cypress and palm leaves
the only sign of the breeze
as the cool of dawn
makes way for
the heatwave
the milkman
returning revellers
the tug boat skipper
all bear witness
to this quiet exchange.

ATHENA

Athena is sleeping far beneath
the bow, among slow, flowing
ribbons of golden kelp and
probing octopi.

A sight to stir a storm among
the shoals of dead sailormen,
otherwise sightless and flaccid
in their search for her.

Poseidon drowns in wet dreams,
pursued by Leviathan and a
stream of mermaids, screaming
'kill the old man of the sea!'

Echoes of the lost and songs of
whales serenade ships without
names, while Athena lies alone
in the company of waves.

Swung to heavy anchors and
laden with strife. Without an
utter of sales, Athena sighs and
waits for the turning tide.

BETTER STILL

there's something
so cathartic about revenge
against your lies
better than the forgiveness
better than gouging out
your lying eyes
better still
the dirty surprise.

BILL EVANS

shed door open
the sound of a plane
drowns out Bill Evans
momentarily, like hope
on this summer night,
lingering, longer
than wine in the glass
and, like the plane,
it will pass, leaving
me alone, interrupted
by intermittent pain.

BLACK FOX

Did the compass of your soul point you,
in this astronomical twilight,
toward the magnetic field
of my deep melancholic state?

Do you believe and feel as I surely do,
that this strange encounter,
this unlikely rendezvous
is not coincidence, but fate?

Our eyes meet through the bars
of this basement kitchen window.
You all coiled up; emaciated
streak of menace.

Once warm cinnamon bleached
by the cold light of the moon.
Black fox; creeping
beneath the trellis.

One who is free from the prison
of emotional wreckage.
One deprived of sleep; senses as
ragged as your ears.

Did the aching of my broken heart,
the hopeless lonely rhythm,
bring you from a distance
through the night to here?

BOURDOIR

candle smoke, sandalwood
and pools of Persian rose oil
in the original Chinatown.
Babylon Bob and his Savannah
Raja, sink into a golden tussled
cushion on their bamboo throne
gazing up at the moon. The king
of Queensway and his queen; she
sipping carnation milk from a
china plate, and he gin from a glass
scented with opium. This is their
courtyard, their royal boudoir.

BRUTUS

Where are you?
Do you wait, as I
do, frozen to the
bone? Or does your
blood run hot in
your heart of stone?

Brutus, by any
other name would
be a sport; a game.
But you and I, Pike,
are enemies and
this is war.

Assassin, torpedo,
ghastly projectile
under the boat.
Ghost in the grime
of the stinking
Mile House cut

Just wait until
the lure sticks in
your throat and
the steel of the
fishmongers knife
opens your gut.

Brutus, my wife,
is bored and lonely,
and my children
poor and fatherless
due to the wretched
things we do.

Come out from
your shopping trolley
cage; Brutus take the
bait, swallow the bitter
hook and put an end
to this age.

CENTRAL WASH

I've seen a kid with blood on his shirt
down at the Central Wash.

I've seen a woman with beautiful curves
down at the Central Wash.

I've seen lost souls killing time
down at the Central Wash.

I've looked inside this heart of mine
down at the Central Wash.

There's a man who can't forget
down at the Central Wash.

There's a woman with many regrets
down at the Central Wash.

There's a baby boy all dressed in blue
down at the Central Wash.

There's a penny for every memory of you
down at the Central Wash.

I wish I could wash away my fears
down at the Central Wash.

I wish I could dry your tears
down at the Central Wash.

I wish we could find healing inside
down at the Central Wash.

I wish for many things tonight
down at the Central Wash.

CIRCUS GIRL

He walked two miles
from the island to
Blackheath in the
pouring rain. Just
to catch a glimpse
of the circus girl -
'cause loneliness
ain't got no shame.

He walked beneath
autumn's low arches
on the hill above the
Thames. Saw General
Wolfe alone and cold
talking to the crows -
'cause loneliness
ain't got no friends.

He reached the heath
as the sun broke free
and saw tent flags
flying in the breeze.
Behind trucks and rides
a golden ticket stand -
'cause loneliness
makes a man believe.

He smelled mud and
tasted diesel and heard
screams and an angel
choir. And when he
saw her his heart raced
as time stood still -
'cause loneliness
heightens desire.

CRUSH

what is this magic, this spell
lifting my gaze, to your golden light
that weaves through invisible worlds
the way the day sneaks up on the night
what is this feeling, this force
leaving my breathless mouth ajar
sending my drooling mind into a trance
as I stare at your face from afar
when did I become so acutely aware
of your kiss-me lips, your sun-warmed hair
falling softly to your shoulders, exposed
gold, beneath the silk blouse
why now after all this time, and opportunity
deserted by even a spark, and me so oblivious
to your sexiness, your selflessness
am I being rearranged by a crush?

DANCERS IN THE GARDEN

Lovers have become dancers in the garden
wet with virus to prevent the ardent embrace.
Hummingbirds still reach deep inside flowers
to lick the nectar, as I long for your mouth
on mine, to feel, but not taste, your lips behind
the gossamer mask on your face. The garden, like
our minds, is a chaos. Fire breaking in upon it,
as we struggle to gain control with our will,
desperate for the human touch, and the end of
the pathogen that separates, divides and kills.

DAUGHTER OF AMPHITRITE

I shall never get you to concentrate entirely on things not concerned with the boat of heaven - your obsession. To plough through the milk of paradise; longboat pushing on proud through Nymphaea floating on the surface, lily pods spreading, their gossamer mouths open.

Vulva, the horn; the ripe wet twat of ocean. And the captain; the fat serpent, single eyed without expression, rises from below, as the promise of blood rushes new life across the veins. His eager cry "plow the flowers, row hard and wet the timber" resonate deep within and set the depths aquiver.

Even when you are drowning in your lustful desire, seasick and drenched to the bone, and the serpent captain is spent; lifeless - a fat cock splayed between open thighs. Even then, when you are faced with waves as high as a wall, I cannot get you to concentrate entirely on a calling higher than the juice in your balls.

So you will fall and I will rise; daughter of Amphitrite, my ocean, leaping and wide, welling and swelling and glorious as you are lost in the tide.

ENCOUNTERS

What if we were meant for each other?
Designed to fit together
To love one another
You and I
Strangers on the train.

What if I am the one for you?
Made to hold you close
Keep you safe
You and I
Shadows in the rain.

What if the universe brought us here?
To this sacred place
This holy hour
You and I
Not to meet in vain.

What if somehow the moment passed
The connection failed
True love slipped away
You and I
Losers of the game.

What are these strange encounters?
The magnetic glances
Ghosts of chances
You and I
Lives yet to rearrange.

EXOTIC ELISE

I thought about you today, as I drove through the old place
The summer of '83? The year of your liberation? I was sixteen.
You were the spring fete queen.
Discovered by someone shooting a movie on location.
Through a gap in the door of the fetish boutique.
They caught a glimpse of your naked figure, half hidden by
cheap rose curtains.
Just a peek. Barely a reflection in that smoke stained mirror.
And now, years later, still the stage lights glow, with their
particular sorrow.
I'm writing a part for you. And you ask me if I could make
it more erotic, please.
Could I? Yes, a thousand times more, my wonderful exotic
Elise.

FEBRUARY

The light is still a supplicant
to winter. It creeps, humble
and low, barely penetrating
the surface; not daring to linger
longer than the season permits.

Water ripples and dances
in defiance. As if in resistance
to the dock's icy grip, but this
is merely shadow play; a thing
less easy than it seems.

Reflection is not for dreamers
of spring. It is for harsh truth
and the admission of sin; so
February just waits, uncaring,
intent and crueller still.

FLITTERMOUSE

I followed her, past cottages clad in larch boards stained black.
Over slimy cobbles, under low steel bridges; rivets like
leeches swelled with diesel. On slug infested, nettle lined
paths above electrified tracks.

By the side of the ancient, suffocating iron oxide deep canal.
Behind walls of jagged clammy stone; the stinking alleyway
reeked of decay. And sorrowful rats, crawled the remains of
the Railwayman.

She moved quickly, and I laboured to keep up with her flight.
It was like following an apparition; her nymph-like frame lit
by a hurricane lamp. We moved in shadows and flickers of
darker light.

We crossed the road, pursuer and pursued, at a hellish pace.
Into the woods and down into the cut; leaving the natural
world far behind. As we reached the bottom not even a strip
of sky remained.

No sound could penetrate, or escape, and no breeze filtrate.
Sunlight never found its way; or wished to inhabit this awful
place. The foreboding atmosphere filled my lungs with a
putrid taste.

It was here, in this natural dungeon, that she now stood still.
Lamp in one hand and a small box in the other; dwarfed by
imposing architecture. Ramparts before the entrance to a
disused black tunnel

For a moment I froze, held by the unspeakable power of a spell.
At once suffocated and invigorated; the chill in the air
stunned my senses. I had lost sight of heaven to walk here,
between iron rails to hell

She walked slowly towards the gaping mouth of the underworld. I edged, crouching low, like a cat; creeping in and out of shallow high arches clothed in pungent fern. All around me, drama began to unfurl.

To my surprise she placed the box on the floor and opened the lid. I was shocked to see several albino rats spill out; scurrying away to follow the line of rusted iron tracks. Crisscrossing sleepers and slipping through cracks.

And then, by far the strangest thing that I have ever seen, happened. More than I had witnessed; in a lifetime of cat and mouse. She began to wave her hurricane lamp and cry "flittermouse, flittermouse, come out of your house."

Dropping my fear, I began to observe what was going on around me. Allowing things to unfold, I dropped to one knee; straining my eyes in the half-light of the abandoned railway cut, I felt butterflies in the pit of my gut.

Three hundred feet or so inside the tunnel there lived a creature. The resident of the old underpass; hanging like a young rabbit from the wet, cold wall. It pricked up its large rodent like ears on hearing her call

At first, I thought I was seeing a stone, and then a ghastly bird. As the creature came hurtling forth; its wings stretching to nearly half a metre, I realised I was seeing a bat, a great mouse-eared web winged creature.

It climbed upward in an arc then descended earthwards in the half-dark. Flapping its wings very slowly as it covered the ground; then flopping on to the track, wings outstretched to fold over its prey, one of the rats.

And, as she softly applauded, I swear on my life and that of my own. That the creature looked back, as if to say thank you; and then once again flew into its dark abode, leaving me aghast, I barely noticed the woman turn and head home.

What would I tell her poor husband of the findings of my investigation? Surely better this strange tale then what he had feared; or maybe not, as some truths are perhaps too weird to be believed. And of course, there is my reputation.

FROM THE EAST

Your upturned face
is the sun, resting
on me, as we lie,
in lamplight - the moon
- penetrating the darkness
of cascading rivers of
midnight blue and bronze
-your hair - and my fingers
searching for the contours
of the earth - your head -
and in your eyes - jewels
in the night - that familiar
look of determination to
enter the meditative place.

GHOST WINDOW

I have heard Leviathan, the sea monster,
glide in the dark places beneath the open
mouth of the Great Serpent, the Thames.

And shivered in the shadow of the unfurled
wings of Halpas, the giant demon stork, as
sailors take warning in the red sky morning.

I have seen fear in the eyes of mudlarkers,
who ventured too far down certain
slipways and saw the underworld lights.

And felt the presence of the ghost of
William Kidd, and heard his gibbet chain
scrape the cobble lanes behind Execution Dock.

But nothing can compare to the blasphemous
whispers of the being which sits on the roof
of the Old Forge, somewhere above the aperture.

The blood-curdling scream of a fallen angel,
haunted by memories of a mad half-existence
before the inner worlds of hell were made.

What power made this hideous apparition
ascend to the layers of heaven, from the
eternal inferno, to the ghost window?

HAWK

Hawk, great hunter of the sky.
Your creator must have painted
you in the fall; brown and red.

Almost invisible to the naked eye.
Behind the crimson burning bush,
a silent cry; wings of lead.

Among lesser splendid things.
Old plant pots, worn out decking,
pea gravel and a broken broom.

Human, cat and pigeon.
Quietly contemplating the arrival
of rain; coming very soon.

A glimmer of electricity.
And we silently count down
until the thunder is here.

The hunchback cat is rigid
And the pigeon paralysed; a gargoyle
on the roof, struck by fear.

And now the sky darkens.
The palm tree moves; leaves like
knives preparing for a fight.

As hailstones fall we hide.
The ice bullets ricochet off
the roof and wall.

Hawk has vanished.
Out of sight, but grounded
from flight still.

And we wonder if Hawk is ill.
Wounded, or tired; or only
seeking shelter from the storm.

HEATWAVE

In this heatwave, I went out walking.
Flip-flop across East London streets
and distant night.

Flip-flop down the boxing club alley.
Flip-flop past a watching fox
and blinking light.

Flip-flop by dead eyed gnomes.
And worn out roses giving
up the ghost.

Flip-flop, along Whitelegg Road.
The inhabitants languid, low strung
and bittersweet.

Flip-flop, the sound of my feet.
Flip-flop, tempered by the sun on
these endless hot days.

Flip-flop, through the open door.
To lay under thin sheets and hope
for a long downpour.

HOT NIGHT

It is summer on some slow cooling
Corner in east London. A ripple
Of the blue parasol overhead;
The only life as the world otherwise
Stops to catch its breath.

There are those who sleep through
This long hot summer night. A whisper
Of rum and things unsaid;
The drunken barman and his dog
Snoring like pigs.

Tom the painter translucent and
Canvas thin. Cigarette
Burned down to the knuckles;
He tosses and turns in deep
Dreams of shallow girls.

Mrs Priory all alone in the big
House on the corner. Falling softly
Under a Tramadol spell;
Nested like a tiny bird in moth balls
In silk in the old wardrobe.

Newly wedded Mrs Jones wishes
She was still Miss Price. And touches
The cold wall with her painted toes;
Arching her back away from his
Warm beer filled gut.

Cats moan, babies cry, sirens wail.
Bobby Womack on one side of the
Borderline, and across the street;
The sound of Charlie Parker and
The midnight train.

What has become of my life?
I want John Coltrane to give me
Hope. But he is also too lazy to inspire;
And so the question rolls over and
Drifts off with the notes.

Even Luna is subdued tonight.
Languid, sad, and pale. Laying low in a
Foggy shroud: what is all the fuss about?
She asks and slides further
Down into low hazy cloud.

I CAN'T BELIEVE ANYMORE

Ooh babe I can't believe anymore.
Oh babe I can't believe no more.

The traffic lights that used to stay on red forever change
faster than they should for this deserted stretch of road.

And you ask me why I sit in my car parked up in the same
spot by the holiday billboard with the couple walking hand
in hand across paradise cove.

There is nothing left for me here but I stay because the
thought of leaving the memory of us in this place leaves me
cold

So I wind down my window
Feel the rain on my skin
I know that you're long gone
But where to begin?

Ooh babe I can't believe anymore.
Oh babe I can't believe no more.

The Christmas lights left on the broken ride to rust jangle in
the wind with little purpose except to remind me that time
goes around.

Across the street is the cafe where I first told you I loved you
and I ain't been back there for six months even though I've
got vouchers.

And the clockwork gypsy singer with hearts for eyes and a
ring through her nose still sits on my dash but the winder is
broken so she makes no sound.

So I wind down my window
Feel the rain on my skin

I know that you're long gone
But where to begin?

Ooh babe I can't believe anymore.
Oh babe I can't believe no more.

They let me go at the factory because I was drunk every day
during the week of the anniversary of you leaving and it still
hurts badly.

Someone told me to sell the leather coat you got for my
birthday but in the absence of your arms it stays wrapped
around me.

And I even kept the wrapping and the card and still read the
words you wrote listing all the reasons why you loved me
deeply and madly.

So I wind down my window
Feel the rain on my skin
I know that you're long gone
But where to begin?

Ooh babe I can't believe anymore.
Oh babe I can't believe no more.

Time heals wounds they say but I hope time never takes this
pain away because it's the only thing that renews in this
world of decay.

Except the still small soft voice of hope that never stops
calling from the depths of this soul saying believe in the
chance that you said is zero.

Walk in the light says the faded sign outside the church and
the only light I want is your sunshine but on this cloudy day
I wait in vain.

So I wind down my window
Feel the rain on my skin
I know that you're long gone
But where to begin?

Ooh babe I can't believe anymore.
Oh babe I can't believe no more.

IF YOU MUST

Go kick the golden carpet,
if you must. Rake the leaves
with you worn out heels,
disturb the layer of rust.

Wallow in this even tide,
if you must. Drag your hem
through decay, under the moon,
your sun at night

Get high on melancholy,
if you must. The opulent
perfume of spent and
fallen fruit at dusk.

Walk alone in shadows,
if you must. Curse the coming
of winter, for the love
you stole and lost.

JUST ONE KISS

You speak of the nature of love;
of Eros, Philia, and Agape. Of
fine amour and romantic bliss.
You swear you would sacrifice
the physical for spiritual; and
passion you would not miss.
But baby please, just one kiss.
Ready your lips, for just one
kiss. Open your mind for just
one kiss. Be damned with me
in just one kiss. Lose yourself
in just one kiss. Baby, oh baby
just one kiss. Just one kiss.

LAST CHANCE SALOON

She was quoting
the writer Bukowski
when she exclaimed:
I like desperate men
with broken teeth,
broken minds and
broken ways.

But that was then
when she was young
and carefree:
before the surprises,
explosions
and long nights
in the A&E.

Now she's looking
in the last chance saloon
for a clean-shaven boy:
clear eyes and necktie,
good job
and kindness
to consume.

But the clean-shaven
boy is looking for
love without misery:
no ghosts,
no baggage
and no
history.

LIZA PRICE

Oh Liza Price, what can the matter be?
The wind chimes are still. Your crystal ball
is dark. Your children are restless in their
sleep. Five hundred miles away, a perfect
storm is forming in the cold north sea.

Oh Liza Price, what can the matter be?
The marsh reeds are whispering.
The men talk softly. The camp fires burn
low. Three hundred miles away, a storm
tide is surging down the east coast.

Oh Liza Price, what can the matter be?
The wind chimes are tinkling. Your crystal ball
is swirling. The marsh foxes bark. One hundred
miles away, a wall of water is building
in the sea in the dark.

Oh Liza Price, what can the matter be?
Your children have woken. The men sit
silent on the caravan steps. The winter air is
strangely heavy. Fifty miles away,
the storm tide hits the Thames estuary.

Oh Liza Price, what can the matter be?
Distant thunder on a February morning?
The men stand in their doorways now.
Holding their breath. Ten miles away,
the storm tide smashes the sea wall at Erith.

Oh Liza Price, why didn't you see the water
coming? Before it swept across the flood plain,
and the marsh. Before the dogs and the ponies
came running. Before seventeen hundred souls
were swept from their homes.

Oh Liza Price, the world is spinning.
The whirlpool is turning. You fear your
children will drown. But, by the light of
the wolf moon, you watch them escape.
In wheelbarrows, horses, and donkeys,
miraculously finding higher ground.

LOST

My brother is lost, out in the distant sea.
And whatever he sees, in those dark waves,
haunts me whenever I dream. But when he returns,
from the distant sea, I know he will remember me.
Through all of his days and all of my nights,
whatever we have learned, faith will set us free.
Faith and the unbreakable chain, the anchor,
the compass, the lighthouse and the pain.
Love remains the same.

MAN-FISH

The man-fish shifts in the salt marsh sand,
next to the airfield, where too many biplanes
once stalled and tumbled from the skies -
lost forever, under this forgotten riverside.

Semi-immortality. The man-fish is dying
from a wound. We kill things we fear, or
don't understand - it whispers and sighs
as hard rain, like bullets, falls from the sky.

The man-fish can see and navigate through
dark deep sea. Telepathic communication, or
amphibious physiology? Knowledge in sorcery -
and yet, there is no escape from man's illogic.

Here, where the river slows and flows past
the remnants of industry, a small tributary -
a boundary around no-man's land, hides dark
secrets of the Death Marshes' harsh history.

Hospital ships once lay offshore, holding the
dead and dying at bay - smallpox, some say -
their bodies cremated in ovens now overgrown
brick ruins. All that remain. All in vain.

Defined by the dark water that moves around
and through them, the man-fish and the people
who lived and died here will leave little trace -
save for the odd bone left in this godforsaken place.

MANTELPIECE

The ledge above the fire.
Candles. A clock. Ceramic
figurines. Angels and brides.
Memories. On the precipice of life.

What are we? You and I.
And them. Souls or ghosts?
Vapour. The chimney walls.
Here, where cold wind blows.

You know you can hold me
and watch the flames dance
beneath the ornaments and
fragments of a broken home.

There are no secrets here.
No mystery. Just flesh and blood,
and bones. Sheltering. Wondering.
Hoping for the promise of love.

MAPLE

The summer is behind me
and the spring is ahead.
From its roots, the maple
draws fire from the core,
transforming golden leaves
to red.

Through the winter it will cradle
me above the frozen floor.
In crimson dreams,
sleep will be long and deep,
until my blood
has thawed.

MARY-JANE GREY

Her resting place, adorned with iron flowers and butterflies
Once brightly painted in pastel hues,
Faded over time.

Overgrown and unkempt, lost in ragweed and day-lilies
Broken penny cast-iron crosses, orange heads,
In hump-backed ditches.

Morbid curiosity, degenerate heredity, the fear of
imperfection
Human oddities and monsters,
Dream of angelic resurrection.

Beneath broken stone turrets, in still and solemn earth
Under lead, at greater depth,
Never to disturb.

Bones of three legs, twisted spine, a porcelain mask
Over the terrible visage,
Of a backward facing head.

Name and date, once rudely stamped on thin tin plate
Here lie the hideous remains,
Of the freak Mary-Jane Grey.

A century of darkness, of endless moonless nights
Hide the brittle mineral frame,
That time left behind.

What made her human? What hope did she have?
Is this her final resting place?
This long forgotten grave.

MELANCHOLY

What is this loneliness?
A glass over a candle flame?
The emptiness of a forgotten
name? Flamenco Sketches and
the sound of the evening rain,
compete with memories of you
distant, faded but never softened.
So harsh, are the lessons of love:
innocence, betrayal and longing.
A cry to the deaf heavens above:
everything we believed is wrong.
No god, no redemption, no good.

MORAVIA

It started here, one summer; the flowering
of love in the rolling wheat fields of Moravia,
among the budding vines, cornflowers and poppies,
the wild rose hip, and the sweet red cherries.

The softness and sweetness of your lips;
the fruit of the rich earth, born from an ancient
coral sea, now wave upon wave of fertile land,
the plumb coloured hills on the horizon.

Under vast blue skies where the buzzard
glides high above the myriad of small creatures,
the bees and butterflies, the crickets and lizards,
the golden hare and the pheasant.

This is the season of growth, of sun and
warm rain; the turning of the land; from bud
to flower to fruit to harvest; and then sleep again.
Silence and the changing of time and hope.

NIGHT BIRD

I imagined I had slept through the cruellest
season; transported by some magic spell
to escape winter, the pandemic, and raise
the blind to see spring; a new breathe of life.

Instead I saw December cloud on steel cold
turrets above the corporate cells and the lower
dwellings of those who sleep in tinsel adorned
rooms, where festive hope lingers, refusing to go.

And I heard a robin singing; the pied piper of
ghosts in the stillness of the small hours. His
voice, brilliant notes from a penny whistle of hope.
A solitary song, with no other noise to compete.

A song of life, brilliant and sweet; the promise
of Spring, for which we all dream of, even those
who cannot sleep. And even those who softly
weep. Even those who want to be alone.

NIGHTLIFE

Sighs from the world turning black.
White glare, red lights, blue sirens.
Night-cancelling day. Some collapse.
Others shadow play. Bars are magnets.
Shop torsos stare. Air tastes of metal.
And smoke. Some care less. Others hope.
Some sleep. Or cry. Others prowl. Fox.
Rat. Owl. Cat. Human. Ghost. Night life.

NO LAST KISS

We are a river that has run its course,
emptying into the sea, you and me.

Our stream of love came from here,
but will not return again, or even remain.

Once a fiery comet, now a falling star,
extinguished, cast into the abyss.

No drama, no commotion, not even a hiss.
Only deafening silence, no last kiss.

NO RHYME OR REASON

i look at a photograph of you
and still feel butterflies
no mystery, no confusion
a simple fact in the truth and lies.

i heard Chrissie Hynde
sing about the thin line
and read the words of Rumi
about wounds letting in light.

i listened to Arrow Benjamin
say there's something in the middle
and saw the evidence of science
prove the contradiction

you to me are light in the dark
sunshine on snow, melting my heart
i could not live without you if I tried
no rhyme, reason or why.

OBSERVATORY

What can you see
from the observatory?
A hopeful mudlark,
a cormorant,
and a girl in
leopard skin pants.
She sells seven bells
on the foreshore.
'cause her fella
is a loose cannon,
on the river wall.

What can you see
from the observatory?
Two slow barges,
wheeling gulls,
a broken heart
lost in the mud.
He is a sailor forlorn
on the rising tide.
'cause his girl
grew tired of waiting,
on the cold bank side.

What can you see
from the observatory?
A ferry idling,
kids on the pier,
wide eyes and
fairground lights.
A promise worth keeping
like never before.
'cause the carousel
horses are restless,
on the distant shore.

OCTOBER

O the early darkness, the deafening silence
of autumn's reluctant transition to winter
-the hands of time slow, without defiance.

The Earth drifts further away from the Sun.
and summer's leftover dreams are disassembled
- the rite of passage to spring has begun.

ONE WITHOUT

aren't we odd ones
you and I
deaf to our desperate sighs.
we only hear what we want to hear
feel what we want to feel
and yet we want so much more
more than the spent love in
the wine glass on the floor.
oh please, please save me from this fate
rescue me before it's too late
the odd one out
the one without
my soul, it seems
outside of your dreams.

OUTSIDER

Opens reluctantly, lizard eyes, cold
As is his heart, or at least its surface
Glacial protection for a human being
Alien to the healing warmth of sleep
Compelled to pull back the curtain
To check on the night, and watch
Telepathic gargantuan heptapods,
Suffocated by fog, waiting for twilight
In desperation they groan and sprawl
Anchored in ancient abdominal clay
behind the garden wall. Their weight
Of despair, the torment of earthlings
To behold, but not hold, the stars
Or navigate constellations, arranged
By the Father of Gaea, as signposts
For Galactic visitors, to guide their Journey
around this dying world.
The human retreats, behind the curtain
Once again, wishing he was made of
Rock, not flesh. Of light, not bone
Home.

PARADOX

Once, when humans waged war on his kin,
in the ploughlands, sodden with
blood and pathogen.

A ragged silhouette in the ghost moon light,
Fox would cast his cold eye on
the distant city walls.

Behind which his maligned and lost
descendants, would skulk and scavenge
in rat infested halls.

Tired of running from hunting dogs,
sick from pesticides, strychnine
and diseased rabbit skins.

Of this madness, Fox could take no more,
and planned to leave the beleaguered den,
escaping by man-made corridors.

He would follow the canal and railway lines
to the city, to make a new life in the maze
of concrete and wire.

But now, there was a different shadow
on his eyes, a new dead zone, the terror
of a more deadly foe.

Humankind was sick and lay dying, suffocating
and alone, while the descendants climbed dark
staircases, searching for prey in homes.

So Fox stayed in the ploughlands, to help
humankind, by feeding on the rats
that would also survive.

Together, man and fox, would forge
new life out of the virus fire,
nature's paradox.

PLATFORM

platform
shoes and sexy legs and then
when I saw your face
i forgot about the train
standing as still
as the clock you stopped.

POISON

Dolores,
Rita, Emma-Jane,
Tequila, Amelia, Laura.
He remembered all their names.
Their kisses sucked his soul bone dry.
Love potion made from the essence of pure desire.
Sweet lips and swaying hips in the bars of old Shanghai.

REASON

He thought he heard what sounded
like a door slamming
in his head.

It was something Reason used to do
but not now since Reason
was dead.

It could be Hope, losing all control
but lately Hope was missing
after leaving home.

What about Sanity? Prone to fits
and cries. Unlikely, since Reason's
untimely demise.

Maybe it was just the hurricane's roar,
out in the darkness,
outside love's open door.

RIVER

The river is dirty
Where the mermaids embark.
And where the light sails unfurl
The river is dark.
The river is calm
Where the sea monster sleeps.
And where the drunken sailor falls
The sea monster eats.
And when river is full
The bones wash up on the beach.
And as the river retreats
By the sun they are bleached.
The Summer days are hot
But the river is cold.
The Autumn moon is new
But the river is old.
When the Winter ice comes
The river still runs.
When the Spring breeze blows
The river goes slow.

SHADOW TREE

He hears them speak of this
crisis, and that. Hard men.
Unkempt. Brutal. Cynics. Bitter
lips, once bloodied and cracked by
harsh elements, suckling rum from
dark glasses, in the dark front room of
The Ferry House. Lamenting things lost,
forgotten and neglected. Things past.

*You don't know the meaning of
loss*, he thinks. He wants to take
one of them by the neck, and stand
him in front of the bar, and say
"Look in the mirror! There behind the
cornucopia of pleasures." There is no
amount of rum in a man that could
mask the terror, or stop the shivers.

What is the point, he thinks.
A drunken memory, as full as piss
as the bladder lads are. He could
headlock two of them, and drag them
outside, across the cobbles, and down the
draw dock and say, "Look in the water!'
There in the mercury swell, lit by the
Moon. And they would be very afraid.

But, no. He will suck the last of the
rum through clenched teeth and go home,
to the house of veils. Where every mirror
and window, every reflecting surface has
been covered or removed. The house where
light has come to a dead stop. The house
of the man with no reflection; a soul whose
luminescent threads have been undone.

And there is worse to come. More of him to
be undone. Two months ago, while walking in
the summer sun, his shadow disappeared, and
has not returned. He is shadowless, apart from
when he stands in front of the shadow tree.
In the flower garden trails, and the red deer park.
On the hill above The Ferry House, the draw dock,
and the house of veils.

"If you cut down the shadow tree, it will be
The end of me. Oh the end of me. Don't send
The hurricane, or the lightning flame. If you
Destroy the tree it will be the end of me.
Oh the end of me. Watch over the shadow tree,
For me, for me. Keep the sun in the sky and
The clouds away. Let us stand in the clearing,
me and my shadow, and the shadow tree."

SHORELINE

I saw the tapestry
of someone's life
hanging on the sea wall.

Sails of ships like
memories and waves
washed up on the shore.

Stones and discarded
remnants of voyages
of loss and hope forlorn.

We ride the river, the flow
and form cutting through
the landscape of life.

Without foresight and
often beset by lies and
fashioned from dreams.

As the shifting sands
beneath also change to
the commands of the sea.

From the source to the
inevitable chaos of freedom
of you, I and we.

Magnets and undercurrents,
the weight of water
cosmic energy.

SOUND OF THE CITY

i am in tune with the world today
absorbing the healing sounds
of the city.

music of life wash the blues away
'cause i'm sho'nuff done with this
ballad of pity.

someone somewhere is learning
the tuba. those low oompah-oomps
tickle my soul.

the rumble of a plane is a joyous
hallelujah. soothing is the serenade
of the last train home.

let me drift on, and drift on by.
underneath the sounds of the city,
such a sweet lullaby.

SOULS BROKE OPEN

I met a downcast woman from the mountainside,
suffering like me in the valley of broken souls.
Moving closer...I saw ghosts in her eyes
-and then such devastating beauty to behold.
Like me...she had fallen for some of the lies
-we are told, about life, love and happiness.
She had been on the path for a thousand days,
searching for the peace at the deep of herself
...weary from the load she had been carrying.
If, like me, you are looking for the one true way
- to discover the joy found at the heart of serenity
...you need to be self-forgotten - dissolved of you.
Make the depths of the desiring heart your destiny
Broken souls don't get out of here, souls broken open do.

STRANGERS

Is this sadness I see in your face-
or tiredness? Or longing? Strange how
you, a stranger, makes me want to hold
you, cradle your head and feel your black
and gold hair fall across my arms; smell
your perfume and taste the bittersweet
sweat on your pale skin, and gently bite
those downturned lips and caress your neck
with my fingers. Raise me, take me, lift
my soul, give me fire and light my desire.
The strange, intoxicating, liberating dreams
of strangers; unsaid, unrequited and unseen.

SUNFLOWER

Now you sit awkwardly
in our landscape.
Even before autumn rolls in,
your pretty head
is heavy with regret.
I'm not sure if you're
trying to remember,
or forget.

The sun will still rise
in the east.
And the moon will glow,
and stars will fall
into your earth.
But there will be
no tomorrow,
or rebirth.

Tonight the velvet shawl
of summer will fall.
The owl, and vole,
watch you stir
in dreams.
And by dawn
you are gone,
and they will sleep.

TAMESIS

Tamesis is far from home, hunting drunken
Seamen who, lamenting lost money and love
Blindly stagger in shale and rotten driftwood
On the strandline, unaware of her cruel lust.

She is the dark nymph, black heart concealed
Within silver breast. Conceived from medieval
Marsh, from the brackish mudflat underworld;
Born to Old Father Thames, lost cousin of Tiberinus.

Motherless spawn of some conjuring sea witch
Concubine to the naked, filthy guardian of hidden
Scrapes, stagnant pools and grazing marsh ditches.
Tormented by wraiths and dead sailors, unbidden.

Tethered to Old Father Thames' long pungent locks
Away from the briny, braiding channels of the flow.
In the company of dying fish and rotting livestock;
Drowning in marsh oil, where the poison lilies grow.

One stormy night, as her siren song carried away
On the howling gale, and the sea serpent Leviathan
Crashed about in the mouth of the boiling estuary,
A colossal wave reared and surged to the marshland.

Where Tamesis' father once offered up his children
Diphtheria and Cholera to those who lived and worked
On his waters, Leviathan's wave now rearranged, undid
His ghastly work, casting free the tormented daughter.

The wash carried Tamesis out to where the river ran
Free. She sang through the returning sea; a song for
The cormorant, the gulls, the seals, whose fur she
Kissed. And then danced and darted, joyful and serene.

All the way to Greenwich, to the slime coated pier,
Where drunken sailors cursed and pissed ale into the
Sullen depths. Tamesis waited; a shadow just beneath
Slippery boards. Moaning to the sound of unsteady feet.

TATTOO

i went to get a tattoo
to mark the end of you
and I, with needles and dye
considered a compass or ship at sea
or a dagger through the heart of we
an anchor and chain, or mountain
angel, lion, eagle, viking sign
tsunami wave and rising sun
wash away and dry the bones of us
in the end I chose a solitary tear
a shroud of rain, a memory so dear
star, light in my darkest sleep
pain where the soul is skin deep.

THE CONTINUOUS MOVEMENT OF WATER

After she left, which was last August,
time was insufferable; as long and slow
as the river where he laboured, forlorn.

The continuous movement of water,
he thought, was not unlike their love;
inevitably running its course.

He barely said a word these days,
instead, with a heart as heavy as river mud,
he worked from sunrise to sunset.

Muted by tears restrained, a boat hand
dreaming of mermaids beneath the bow wave,
listening for the sound of a flute.

As they sailed past the music school, where
she studied. Her, as distant and transient
as the notes once played.

She cried a lot, throughout September,
and sat by her window, looking for the tops
of boats in shrouds of rain.

She watched water on the roof tiles make
tributaries, before joining the lead gutter to
wash out of sight.

The continuous movement of water,
she thought, was not unlike their love;
inevitably running its course.

She rarely played her flute these days,
instead, with a song as sad as falling leaves
serenading her every thought.

She spent the days drinking warm tea,
and the evenings sipping ice cold gin
from the same china cup.

Water boils, water freezes,
but is never truly contained, like his meandering
mind; never a firm plan constructed.

Him, as fluid as the river on which he glides,
never a course obstructed,
as fleeting as the tide.

THE CORMORANT

It dives through the black and blue
lives of drowning souls and debris
of broken and scattered hopes of
those taken by the infernal flow.

A cormorant hunting the myriad
light creatures of the river wide as
they swarm and ride the magnetic
undercurrent at the Meridian line.

"I am life," cries the cormorant, as
it dives and the light creatures divide
and hide in mud and rocks strewn
along the blackened banks at low tide.

"I am death," cries the cormorant, as
it rises and the light creatures flee for
their lives, like fireflies skimming the
surface, dark water absorbing their light.

The sea absorbs the river, and the next
life absorbs this, creating new light and
new life just as the cormorant rises and
dives and the light creatures live and die.

THE HAPPENING OF MAGIC

A dead tree in Kelsey Park
where a black pigeon sits
in a nook almost invisible
against the bark.

A Robin skims a stream
with a water nymph in
pursuit on wings of
unfolding dreams.

A discarded paper cup
and a butterfly of silver
blue are particles
in the mud.

A white witch on a path
that weaves through purple
hues of sorrel beneath
the oak and ash.

A forbidden kiss and a star
explodes for a wish that may
come true outside the
gates of Kelsey Park.

A place where we hide
from earthly lies and seek
cosmic truth in atoms
that happen to collide.

A dance of energy and trick
of light is the pattern and
design of you and I and
the happening of magic.

THE LOVE EQUATION

she
with the beautiful mind
drew a graph of love
and desire
with a heart curve
and chart showing
interactions and connections
an emotional intersection
and compatibility projection
and plotted the nature
of passions and attraction
reducing lust
to a simple fraction
and her heart
trapped inside her head
longed to draw
this great equation
onto her lover's body
in bed, in wild
anticipation of some kind of
soul salvation.

THE PERSIAN CINDERALLA

Beauty and the beast, he thought, as he lay beside her in the silence of their temple of desire.

He looked at his own reflection in the table mirror. Pot-bellied, gnarled, twisted, bloated, bulbous and scarred.

The small room was musty and slightly damp, with floor-to-ceiling shelves made out of beer crates. Books were stacked and tucked and jumbled in piles.

Why are you here, with me? The question stuck in his throat, like a brazen nail, fixed in the door of consternation.

He was awed by her indescribable beauty, which he could not fathom. His passionate kisses had left their marks on her shoulders. Hers had drawn blood from his lip.

Her skin was as radiant as the sun. I want you, and I know that I can never take you in my arms again, he thought, as he gazed upon her upturned face; golden in the glow of the mosaic hanging lamp that serenaded their unlikely dalliance.

As she slept, her lifted her foot and returned the anklet to its rightful place.

You are like a clear, bright sky. And I am a captive bird in this cage. Let love be stronger than pride—don't forget that: let love be stronger than pride.

THE SLOPE

Nightly beneath the barbed edge rim of suburbia, he walked with a stoop. Under a dome of beech leaves, past stunted pines, and through corridors of wayfaring. Along rough grassed and ox-eye daisy sloping sides of mud streams, and further down towards the dead tree swamp.

Here he stopped, a few metres short of the gravel pit lake, and lay down in the hollow of an old rabbit hole. Hawthorns pricked through tufts of grass, as fresh as the grief, everything sharp around the edges. As the sun dipped below the horizon, and memory rose like a pike from the cold depths.

Now, exploding in the reed beds, the scales of the reaper bearing weights of guilt and anger, became an anchor to his head. He turned sideways and watched tiny figurines of white orchids angled towards one another, whispering in the breeze.

He saw the reflection of the rising new moon in the dark water, the outline of concrete and fallen trees, and the tip of an old hay conveyor, lost like a wreck at sea. Destruction is not always followed by new life, he said, as the last rays of light surrendered to the night.

He closed his eyes, and thought of his son, drowned and not long dead, expired but not erased. Not as a supplicant did he come to this place, but as one who demanded to end his life the same. He pulled himself up, and considered the walk home. But shorter still was the slope, the deep, and hope.

THE SOLDIERS RETURN

A cold, damp and heavy December day,
all mood light on hope, crawling into city smoke.
The train brakes to stop, fast as ever is the clock
as lovers are never outside, so the long low porch
again hides forsaken souls as raw and bare as
scattered bones on the battlefield that took the life
of many a friend. Straightening his cap and crumpled
brow, lest it should offend, he wonders how many others
might hide what they secretly yearn, and how many will,
in time, count the cost of the soldiers return.

THE SUPPLICANTS

Whether they served a purpose or wasted away,
the lines of sunflowers sit before Dionysus
as supplicants; lesser inhabitants of the fields.

Why wait for him to pass by? When all He cares
for is the intoxication of the wine; the gift
from His most beloved vine.

For twenty days of splendid full bloom, in sun
and moon, every waking hour, waiting, praying, for
Him to enjoy the beauty of their flower.

But summer came and went and in the absence
of the autumnal god their heads bent, toward the
soil cooling, hardening, the life-force now spent

Colour fading. The disenchanted glower of those
overlooked, neglected, left behind.
This is the fall, the resting of the land.

There is no reclamation for them. No late harvest.
And even if the season drags it's feet, or winter
beats a temporary retreat,

Dionysus will not offer so much as a helping hand.
Live and die, in the lines where you stand.
Live and die at His command.

THE WALK

He left his house before dawn
as quiet as a cat
and slinking like a scolded hound
slipping the lock without a sound.

Leaving her under the heavy quilt
honeypot and pouting lips
out into the heavy morning dew
burdened by the things he knew.

He walked a mile to Blackwell farm
tasted the rank silage musk
saw cattle in dirty ploughed fields
plastic sugar-beet sacks and winter wheat.

He sat beneath a fat gnarled oak
under a running sky
bleeding rays of the sun's early warning
wishing the crows would carry away his scorn.

There is nothing here but shit and strife
and heartless working land
and he thought of Elijah's shattered focus and faith
and the moment of its leaving when loves turns to hate.

THIS IS LOVE

Will you follow me?
From your high castle
to my low shed.
From your rich paradise
to my poor distress.
From your sumptuous boudoir
to my mattress on the floor.
From your aristocracy
to my mediocrity.
Can you sacrifice?
Will love suffice?

THROUGH THE EYES OF LOVE

Under the cedar, ten minutes into my meditation
-everything dissolving, breath and mind in fusion.
An incredible being of love and light - an angel or
some alien - disguised in the form of a human appeared,
and without speaking said, "through the ages and in
each moment, man has looks through the lens of
judgement and fear, gazing down - rooted to the ground
..head bent to the world, never looking above or beyond
self - never looking or seeing through the eyes of love
always reaching, always searching, lost but never found.
Always looking through the eyes of love, all fear expelled
- so every moment becomes a gift, and all that remains
is the power of your spirit, of your limitless self.

TIGRESS

On the road to a village in Nepal,
I met a traveller, a learned man,
who spoke of a shaman hunting a
tigress, the man-eater Binsa Khan.

He told me a tale so strange, it was
hard to believe. But, compelled, I
followed him to a farmers hut, where,
from a distance, we secretly watched.

The shaman, standing in a sugar cane
field. A smoky lantern, and incense box,
attached to a pole, which the shaman
swung high, while calling Binsa Khan.

And to our surprise, and alarm, the tigress
suddenly appeared, and lay down at his feet.
Apart from our wildly beating hearts, all
was strangely and hypnotically calm.

For half an hour, they remained in this pose,
until, without warning, the man-eater arose,
turned and disappeared, and with her our prayers
for the shaman answered if not heard.

TORN DOWN

He passes out before the light of dawn
after drinking a flagon of rum.
And wakes with pain behind his eyes,
white hot in the afternoon sun.

Oh oh she has torn him down
from the cradle of love
to the dust of the ground.
And all he knows
is a soul can be cold
in the fire of abandonment.

He lies on a bed of disbelief
Heaving to the poison of lies.
And spits out each one in turn
Like a swarm of angry flies.

Oh oh she has torn him down
From the cradle of love
To the dust of the ground.
And all he knows
Is a soul can be cold
In the fire of abandonment.

He tosses and turns and curses
Howling at the heartless moon.
And sleeps with a fever that boils
Like poison on a dirty spoon.

Oh oh she has torn him down
From the cradle of love
To the dust of the ground.
And all he knows
Is a soul can be cold
In the fire of abandonment.

TRANSIT

The ghost of you
is vapour now;
passing clouds
in a dark sky.

As vacuous as the
look in your eyes.
And so, at night,
the rails I ride.

Away from the hate
and lies. Better to
roam, to be in transit,
free if not alone.

I, on this outside loop,
never to darken your
door. For you and I,
there is no more.

UNEXPLODED BOMB

There is an unexploded bomb
In the mud, on the foreshore
At the foot of the old ramp
That is Johnsons Drawdock.

A mudlark found it, as she
Combed the naked river bed
For lost coins, not death's debris
Shifting in silt, rearing its head.

Skywards, where it once flew
From the bomber's open grip
Above the U of the Great Serpent,
The mighty executor of ships.

Before it settled, unspent and unlit
For eighty years in shallow depths
Iron heart stopped where it sits
Comatose and cold, not quite dead.

And now, they pray. Mudlark and
Other spectators, on the wall above
Johnsons Drawdock. Bated breath
Waiting for the army bomb squad.

The river bus and the tugs sail past
Slowly, on the other side, but the
Wash still breaks on the foreshore
Where the unexploded bomb lies.

And then, a cormorant lands on
The fin of the once dormant device
Even the gulls are mute. The police
Boat without a siren. Silence.

Never has the Great Serpent appeared
So still. In her belly, a wingless bringer
Of death. It's cruel heart still beating
A dark memory now awakening.

Omitting a shriek, the cormorant dives
The harbinger of chaos. No one hears
What it heard, the low tick of an old
Mechanical clock. The beast is alive.

And the Great Serpent sinks and rises
The earth moves underneath the mudlark
And violently divides. The device has returned
To life in the mud at Johnsons Drawdock.

WINTER TWILIGHT MAN

Softly in the Winter twilight,
before the workers hurry home
grubby collars turned up, hats pulled
down and tired limbs chilled to the bone.

I heard you singing Spanish Ladies,
in a low melody, sitting on top of a sewer,
impervious to the cold
above the East London cemetery.

I used to see you, out walking
with a small old pug
from the Lea and Bow Bank rivers,
at the edge of Hackney

and then breathless by the trackside scrub.
Where's the little fella, I asked reaching out
an earnest hand. A fiver for his coffer, and
leaning close I heard him whisper
He passed to the Summer land.